Moscow Mule Recipe Book

38 Best Moscow Mule Variations You Should Learn to Make

Copyright © 2023

DEDICATION

Contents

Classic Moscow Mule

Before we get into all the fantastic variations of this tasty summer cocktail, let's start with the basics.

You'll love this classic Moscow mule recipe for its ease and simplicity. And if you're a purist at heart, it's by far the best of the bunch.

For the tastiest Moscow mule around, use Titos and Fever-Tree (vodka and ginger beer).

Oh, and always use fresh lime juice!

❖ Ingredients

2 ounces (¼ cup) vodka

½ ounce (1 tablespoon) fresh lime juice

4 ounces (½ cup) ginger beer

For the garnish: lime wheel or wedge, fresh mint (if desired)

❖ Directions

Step 1: Pour the vodka, lime juice, and ginger beer into a copper mug.

Step 2: Add ice and garnish with a lime slice. Serve immediately.

Strawberry Moscow Mule

A joyful summertime treat mixed with alcohol. This Moscow mule recipe uses sweet strawberries that set off the ginger beer's spiciness amplified with a black pepper sprinkle.

❖ Ingredients

4 - 5 oz. Ginger beer

2 oz. Vodka

½ oz. Lime juice

2-3 Large fresh strawberries or 5-6 tiny ones, stems removed and sliced, one reserved for garnish

1 or 2 Cranks of fresh black pepper (optional)

❖ How to Make

Using a muddler, smash the strawberry slices with lime juice in a shaker tin.

Add vodka.

Add ice and shake well.

Strain mixture into your chilled copper mug filled with ice.

Pour ginger beer over the vodka mixture.

Garnish with a strawberry.

If you want to add a complex touch, finish the drink off with a couple of fresh black pepper cranks. This adds a deep flavour that brings out the slight sweetness of the strawberries.

Pineapple Moscow Mule

Pineapple is the most popular tropical fruit because not only is it delicious, it is also very healthy and versatile to use. The vodka, ginger beer, lime juice, and pineapple juice combination are refreshing and a great drink, especially during the summer.

❖ **Ingredients**

Ice

2 oz. vodka

2oz Dole 100% Pineapple Juice

1 oz lime juice

Zevia Mixer Ginger Beer

❖ How to Make

Fill a copper mug with ice.

Add the vodka, pineapple juice, and lime juice.

Top with ginger beer and stir.

Garnish with a pineapple wedge, a ginger crystallized candy and mint sprigs.

Georgia Mule Recipe (Peach and Ginger)

The reason ginger beer works so well for the Moscow mule is that it has a nice fiery kick that you just can't get with ginger ale. But sometimes even ginger beer isn't hot enough. When you find yourself longing for a southern-style combo, this peach and ginger-enhanced Moscow mule recipe is a perfect choice.

❖ Ingredients

For the drink:

4-5 oz. Ginger beer

1.5 oz. Vodka

1 oz. Ginger-peach puree

Fresh peach slices for garnish

Candied ginger for garnish

For the ginger-peach puree:

2-3 Large ripe peaches (with thin slices for garnish reserved) pitted and cut in half

1 One-inch piece of fresh ginger (skin removed)

¼ cup Lemon juice

¼ cup Water

2 tbsp Honey (more to taste if peaches are tart)

❖ How to Make

Make the peach puree by adding all ingredients to the blender and puree until smooth. Taste and adjust flavours as needed (ginger for more heat, peaches and honey for more sweetness, lemon juice for more sourness). Strain well using a fine strainer and discard all solids.

Add the ginger-peach puree and vodka into a cocktail shaker filled with ice and shake well.

Strain the ginger-vodka mixture into a copper mug filled with ice.

Pour ginger beer over the vodka mixture until the cup is full.

Garnish with thin peach slices and candied ginger.

Skinny Mule

A Moscow mule may be worth the calories, but sometimes we must give in to self-control. A low-sugar, low-calorie classic Moscow mule recipe doesn't have to be the fantasy of your late-night cravings.

❖ **Ingredients**

4-5 oz. Ginger beer

1.5 oz. Organic vodka

½ oz. Lime juice

❖ How to Make

Squeeze lime juice into a copper mug filled with ice.

Add organic vodka.

Fill the rest of the cup with ginger beer.

Garnish with a half lime wheel.

Pomegranate Mule

If the floral note of the hibiscus-berry mule isn't your style, try this pomegranate Moscow mule recipe variation instead. It's just as bold and red but uses the tartness of pomegranate instead of floral hibiscus.

❖ Ingredients

4-5 oz. Ginger beer

1.5 oz. Vodka

½ oz. Pomegranate juice

½ oz. Lime juice

Fresh pomegranate seeds for garnish

Lime wedge for garnish

❖ How to Make

Combine pomegranate juice, vodka, and lime juice into a copper mug filled with ice.

Pour ginger beer over the vodka mixture until the cup is full.

Garnish with pomegranate seeds and a lime wedge.

Mule Driver (Orange and Ginger Combo)

This gingery cousin to the college-classic screwdriver is enough to drive away every bad memory you have of waking up hungover on a friend's couch. Delicious and refreshing, you can have this orange and ginger beer combo Moscow mule recipe any time of day.

❖ **Ingredients**

4-5 oz. Ginger beer

1.5 oz. Vodka

1 oz. Orange juice

½ oz. Lime juice

Orange slice for garnish

❖ How to Make

Combine orange juice, vodka, and lime juice into a copper mug filled with ice.

Pour ginger beer over the vodka mixture until the cup is full.

Garnish with slices of orange and lime.

Kentucky Bourbon Mule

Kentucky can say that the Kentucky mule is their pride and joy. It takes bourbon, mixed with a spicy ginger beer and the tang of lime and that becomes an awesome drink. Will it be as good as vodka used in the original mule? Give it a try and decide for yourself.

❖ **Ingredients**

2 oz. Woodford Reserve Kentucky Bourbon

½ oz. freshly squeezed lime juice

Fentimans Ginger beer (to top)

Sprig of mint (for garnish)

Ice cubes

❖ Directions

Squeeze the lime using a citrus squeezer and measure it as well as the bourbon with a jigger and pour them into a copper mug.

Fill the copper mug with ice cubes.

Top it off with ginger beer and stir with the bar spoon.

Lightly slap the sprig of mint against your hand to open up the aroma and garnish it on the drink.

Garden Mule

This jazzed-up version of the mule calls for the vodka but also works well with gin or tequila. In addition to ginger beer and lime juice, this interpretation of the Moscow mule recipe requires some flavour-enhancing accoutrements.

❖ Ingredients

4 Slices cucumber

16 Blueberries

6 Mint leaves and sprig for garnish

2 oz. Vodka

1 oz. Lime juice

½ cup Ginger beer

1-piece Candied ginger

❖ How to Make

Take a cocktail shaker and put cucumber, 8 blueberries, and mint leaves in the bottom.

Muddle until the whole concoction is crushed and appears juicy.

Add ice, lime juice, and vodka.

Shake for 10-15 seconds.

Put ice in the copper mug and strain the liquid into it.

Now, add ginger beer and 4 blueberries.

Cut open the remaining 4 blueberries and candied ginger using a toothpick and use it alongside a sprig of mint.

Mint Moscow Mule

When you watch videos on how to make Moscow mules, this cocktail is presented with a sprig of mint leaves as a garnish. But mint is such a powerful ingredient that you can incorporate in the cocktail rather than mere decoration.

❖ Ingredients

1.5 oz. Vodka

6-8 Mint leaves

1 Whole fresh lime juice

1 Sugar cube

2 oz. Ginger beer

Crushed Ice

A sprig of mint leaves (for garnish)

❖ How to Make

In a copper mug, put in the sugar cube. Squeeze the lime with a citrus squeezer straight into the mug.

Muddle the combined ingredients gently for about 5 seconds. Add the mint leaves and give it two twists with the muddler.

Measure the vodka and ginger beer using a jigger and pour them into the copper mug.

Stir the contents gently using a bar spoon. Then, add the crushed ice to the top of the mug.

Finally, garnish it with a sprig of mint leaves.

Moonshine Mule

Everyone buys a jar of moonshine if they visit Kentucky. And this is one of the best ways to use it up when you get home.

This moonshine mule recipe provides the perfect combination of gingery citrus with a powerful kick!

If you find vodka isn't quite strong enough, this is the drink for you.

❖ Ingredients

1 knob fresh ginger peeled and roughly sliced

2 oz moonshine

fresh ice

4 oz ginger beer

lime for garnish

❖ Directions

Step 1: In a copper mug, muddle the fresh ginger.

Step 2: Next add the moonshine, ice and fill the remainder of the mug with ginger beer, approximately 4 oz.

Step 3: Garnish with a lime.

Molly Sims' Skinny Moscow Mule

Are you trying to cut sweeteners from your diet? Then this Skinny Moscow Mule is the cocktail you've been dreaming about! We love a tasty Moscow Mule, Kentucky Mule, or any kind of ginger beer cocktail.

❖ Ingredients

2 cups Sparkling ginger-flavored soda water

1 cup Vodka

1 cup Chilled green tea

1/2 cup Lime juice

1 tsp Grated peeled fresh ginger

4 slices Peeled fresh ginger

4 Thin lime slices

Ice

Fresh mint leaves

❖ Directions

Step 1: Muddle vodka, green tea, and lime juice with grated and peeled ginger.

Step 2: Pour over ice and top with ginger-flavored soda water.

Step 3: Serve with fresh mint leaves as garnish.

Step 4: Servings

Mexican Mules

As a massive margarita lover, this is one of my favorite Moscow mule variations. And it's especially delicious with the spicy garnish! You'll use tequila instead of vodka, which adds a little more flavor and complexity to every sip.

But the key ingredient here is the jalapeño garnish. Trust me, it's a must!

The spiciness mixes so perfectly with the heat of the ginger beer. It's such a fun twist on the typically clean classic.

❖ Ingredients

2 oz tequila blanco

1 tablespoon lime juice ½ lime

4 oz ginger beer

❖ Directions

Step 1: Fill a copper mug or highball glass with ice

Step 2: Pour in the tequila and lime juice

Step 3: Top up the mug or glass with ginger beer

Step 4: Garnish with jalapeno slices, if desired and lime wedges

Jalapeño Moscow Mule

Now, here's a rendition you've gotta try! And no, there's no tequila in this recipe.

Instead, you'll use a mix of gin, jalapeños, and ginger beer. Each element brings an enjoyable mouthfeel, making your palate crave more.

It's refreshing, cool, and loaded with fun flavors. No deck lounging is complete without a tumbler full of this bright drink.

❖ Ingredients

¼ cup fresh mint sprigs

1 thinly sliced jalapeño (divided)

¼ cup lime juice

6 ounces gin (or vodka)

12 ounces ginger beer

Simple syrup to sweet (optional)

❖ Directions

Step 1: In a pitcher, use the back of a wooden spoon to muddle together the mint, half of the jalapeño slices and lime juice.

Step 2: Pour in gin then stir well.

Step 3: Fill four copper mugs with ice and add in equal parts of the gin mixture leaving filling the mugs 3/4 of the way full.

Step 4: Top off each glass with equal parts ginger beer and serve with additional jalapeño slices or lime wedges for garnish.

Strawberry Moscow Mule Recipe

If you love a cold glass of strawberry limeade on a humid day, you'll go nuts for this adult version.

Can you think of a better combination than strawberry, lime, and ginger beer?

Each sip is so fruity and tart that you won't want to share

❖ Ingredients

4 - 5 oz. Ginger beer

2 oz. Vodka

½ oz. Lime juice

2-3 Large fresh strawberries or 5-6 tiny ones, stems removed and sliced, one reserved for garnish

1 or 2 Cranks of fresh black pepper (optional)

❖ Directions

Step 1: Using a muddler, smash the strawberry slices with lime juice in a shaker tin.

Step 2: Add vodka.

Step 3: Add ice and shake well.

Step 4: Strain mixture into your chilled copper mug filled with ice.

Step 5: Pour ginger beer over the vodka mixture.

Step 6: Garnish with a strawberry.

Peach Moscow Mule

I think peach and ginger beer go together like peas and carrots.

The sweetness of peach is accentuated by the spice of the carbonated

ginger beer, creating a unique experience you'll swoon over. Delight your dinner guests by concocting this fantastic cocktail. Trust me, you won't regret it.

❖ Ingredients

8 oz peach vodka

24 oz ginger beer

4 oz lemon juice, fresh squeezed

¼ cup fresh basil

❖ Directions

Step 1: Fill four glasses with ice. Preferably copper cups, but any cocktail glass will work.

Watermelon Moscow Mule

Any cocktail with watermelon is a win in my book.

I mean, how can you beat pink sugary sweetness combined with ice and liquor?

And all you have to do is blend the fruit and add it to a classic Moscow mule recipe. How easy is that?

Each sip will cool you off and warm you up in the best way possible. Of course, you'll likely need to add a little extra vodka. I suggest tasting it as you go until it's perfect.

❖ Ingredients

⅔ cups seedless watermelon chunks

1 ½ ounces citrus vodka

1 juice of lime wedge

4 ounces ginger beer

watermelon wedge and mint leaves to garnish

ice cubes

❖ Directions

Step 1: Place the watermelon chunks into the pitcher of a blender. Cover and puree until smooth.

Step 2: Strain the watermelon, reserving the juice. Discard the pulp.

Step 3: Place 1/4 cup of watermelon juice, vodka, and lime juice into an ice filled cocktail shaker. Cover and shake to thoroughly combine.

Step 4: Strain cocktail into an ice filled copper mug. Top with ginger beer, and garnish with watermelon wedge and mint sprigs.

Apple Cranberry Mule

This Easy Cranberry Apple Moscow Mule recipe is perfect for

Thanksgiving… or anytime you want a fun Fall cocktail! Made with apple cider, cranberry juice, ginger beer, and bourbon, this drink comes together in seconds. And it's so refreshing! W

❖ Ingredients

1 1/2 oz. vodka

1/2 oz. Monin Apple Syrup

1/2 oz. Monin Cranberry Syrup

1 oz. fresh lime juice

4 oz. ginger beer

Optional Garnishes:

Apple slices

Frozen cranberries

Rosemary Sprigs

❖ Directions

Step 1: Fill a large copper mug or a tall glass with ice.

Step 2: Add the bourbon. Then top with apple cider, cranberry juice, and finally ginger beer.

Step 3: Gently stir, then top with garnishes, if desired. Serve cold, at once.

Blueberry Moscow Mule

This is one pretty drink you'll crave all summer long. There's no denying that the color is the best thing about this drink.

That is… until you take a sip!

And boy, oh boy, is that first sip good! So good, in fact, you'll want a second right away (and a third!).

This striking cocktail will delight your guests and sit gracefully on any patio table.

❖ Ingredients

Fresh or frozen blueberries – Scroll down for more fruity moscow mule versions!

Lime juice

Ginger beer

Vodka

Pure Maple Syrup (optional) – Adds a touch more sweetness and pairs nicely with blueberries

Fresh mint (kind of optional) – It can be left out, but gives it that little nudge for making the best mule!

❖ Directions

Step 1: First muddle some fresh or frozen blueberries in the bottom of the glass or copper mug with a couple mint leaves, lime juice, and maple syrup, if using.

Step 2: Top with ice and then pour in vodka and ginger beer.

Step 3: Give a quick stir and garnish with more blueberries and an additional mint leaf.

Mezcal Mule

I had to include this recipe because I'm a little obsessed with mezcal at the moment.

Its smoky flavor is just so irresistible. And when you mix it with lime juice and ginger beer, it's borderline addictive!

Each sip is bubbly with sweet and tangy flavors. Then you get a smoky aftertaste that'll make your head spin (in a good way). This drink goes down dangerously easy, so make sure to drink responsibly!

❖ **Ingredients**

½ ounce (1 tablespoon) mezcal*

1 ½ ounces (3 tablespoons) tequila

½ ounce (1 tablespoon) fresh lime juice

4 ounces (½ cup) ginger beer

For the garnish: lime slice

❖ **Directions**

Step 1: In a copper mug or glass, pour in the mezcal, tequila, lime juice, and ginger beer.

Step 2: Add ice and garnish with a lime slice. Serve immediately.

Blood Orange Thyme Moscow Mule

If you're looking for an elevated take on this timeless summer drink, here's one recipe you won't forget.

This blood orange and thyme Moscow mule provides a unique

sensory experience for your tongue. And it looks incredible too! Between the deep sweetness of the blood orange and the light herbaceousness of the thyme, your palate will go crazy.

❖ Ingredients

½ cup granulated sugar

½ cup water

5 blood orange slices (optional)

Blood Oranges - The beautiful blood oranges are the star of this cocktail! However, any type of oranges (or other citrus like lemon or grapefruit) would work just as well.

Fresh Thyme - I just love the flavor of fresh thyme with blood oranges, but mint or rosemary would also be delicious!

Simple Syrup - You can add as little or as much simple syrup as you like but it's totally optional if you prefer a more sour cocktail!

Vodka - I used Ketel One Botanicals Peach & Orange Blossom vodka because I had it at home and it was absolutely amazing!! But any regular or citrus vodka would be delicious!

Ginger Beer - Is it even a Moscow mule without ginger beer?? (Not to be confused with ginger ale).

Orange Bitters - I like to add a dash or two of orange bitters to add a bit of complexity and enhance the flavor of the blood oranges, but you can leave them out if you prefer!

❖ Directions

Add the sugar, water, and blood orange slices to a small saucepan over medium heat.

Stir until sugar is completely dissolved.

Let cool completely to room temperature, then strain into a glass jar and seal tightly with a lid.

Store in the fridge for up to a month!

Apple Cider Moscow Mule

Who said Moscow mules are just for summer?

Thanks to this drink recipe, you can enjoy a cool refresher in the winter months too.

If you go crazy for mulled wine, then this recipe will blow your mind.

The ginger beer spice works perfectly with apple cider's subtle warmth. But feel free to add some cinnamon stick too!

You'll complement this dynamic duo with a spritz of lime and vodka for the ultimate cocktail experience. Yum!

❖ Ingredients

4 ounces apple cider

1 ½ ounces vodka

1/4 lime (juiced)

4-6 ounces ginger beer

❖ Directions

Add apple cider, vodka, lime juice and ice to a copper mug. Top with ginger beer to fill. Enjoy!

Mango Moscow Mule

Okay, how does it get any better than this?

Imagine sipping on this delectable drink and having flavors of sweet mango, tart lime, and zingy ginger beer wash over your palate.

Mmm…I'm drooling already!

This is by far the best way to beat the summer heat. So, the next time the forecast is looking a little balmy, keep this invigorating cocktail in mind.

❖ Ingredients

2 ounces vodka

1½ ounces mango juice

1½ ounces fresh-squeezed lime juice

Ginger beer

Lime wheel, for garnish

Mango slice, for garnish

❖ Directions

In a cocktail shaker filled with ice, combine the vodka, mango juice and lime juice. Shake until well-chilled. Strain into a cup mule mug filled with cracked ice. Top with ginger beer. Garnish with a lime wheel and a mango slice.

Irish Mule

If you celebrate Saint Patrick's Day a little closer to the equator, then why not cool off with this Irish mule?

It tastes just like the classic Moscow mule you know and love, but with the added bite of Irish whiskey to keep things interesting.

❖ **Ingredients**

2 ounces irish whiskey

6 ounces ginger beer or more!

Juice of half a lime about 1 ounce

Lime slices optional, for garnish

Mint sprig (optional for garnish

Ice

❖ Directions

Fill a copper mug (or other glass) with ice. Pour in whiskey and lime juice, top with ginger beer. Stir to mix, garnish with lime slices and mint sprig.

Kentucky Bourbon Mule

Nothing makes the Moscow mule a classic American darling than bourbon. Great bourbons are born in Kentucky and bred from the finest American corn. This Moscow mule recipe uses good Kentucky bourbon that compliments ginger beer with vanilla notes for an extra-boozy kick.

❖ Ingredients

4-5 oz. Ginger beer

1.5 oz. Kentucky bourbon

½ oz. Lime juice

Mint sprigs for garnish

❖ Directions

Step 1: Combine bourbon and lime juice in a copper mug filled with ice.

Step 2: Top with ginger beer until the mug is full.

Step 3: Garnish with a lime wheel and mint sprig.

Clementine Moscow Mules

Clementine juice is a legitimately delicious addition to the Moscow Mule, and one that makes the drink seem more seasonally appropriate as we head into Thanksgiving and the winter holiday season.

❖ Ingredients

Juice of 1 clementine

Juice of ½ lime

1 ½ ounces vodka

4 ounces ginger beer

❖ Directions

Step 1: In a cocktail shaker filled halfway with ice, shake clementine juice, lime juice and vodka until ice cold.

Step 2: Strain into a glass (preferably a copper mug) filled about ⅔ full with ice.

Step 3: Top with 4 ounces ginger beer and serve, garnished with clementine or lime if you like.

Raspberry Lime Moscow Mule

If blueberries are too sweet for you, try this raspberry version on for size. It'll knock your socks off with bright, fruity flavors of pure deliciousness.

You'll love this sparkling pink drink for patio hangs with friends when the weather warms up.

I like to use raspberry vodka to boost the flavor. But if they're fresh, real raspberries should be more than enough.

❖ Ingredients

1 half lime (juiced)

10 raspberries

2 ounces vodka

4-6 ounces ginger beer

Fresh mint sprigs (for garnish)

❖ Instructions

Muddle lime juice and raspberries in a copper mug. Add vodka and ice to fill and top off with ginger beer. Enjoy!

Maple Moscow Mule

With the warm fall afternoons making us want to spend a lot of afternoons out enjoying the colors, we figured a nice cool sipping drink would be appropriate, so we came up with the Maple and Cider Kentucky Mule.

❖ Ingredients

2 ounces Kentucky Bourbon

2.50 ounces apple cider

.75 ounce maple syrup

.50 ounce freshly squeezed lime juice

3 ounces ginger beer

❖ Directions

Step 1: Combine all ingredients over crushed ice in a copper mug.

Step 2: Stir to combine.

Step 3: Garnish with crystallized ginger and an apple slice if desired.

Cherry Moscow Mule

This Cherry Moscow Mule puts a delicious spin on the traditional moscow mule. Fresh cherries, lime juice, vodka and ginger beer are all you need to make this delicious, icy and refreshing cocktail. We've got just a little over a month of summer left – Let's make the most of it by celebrating with these Cherry Moscow Mule cocktails! These are definitely being added to our Labor Day menu this year – They're the perfect blend of sweet and tangy, icy and refreshing, and the little drops of condensation on those copper mugs just win my heart every time.

❖ Instructions

1 half lime juiced

6 cherries (pitted)

2 ounces vodka

4-6 ounces ginger beer

Fresh mint sprigs for garnish

Lime wheels (for garnish)

❖ Directions

Muddle lime juice and cherries in a copper mug. Add vodka and ice to fill and top with ginger beer. Serve garnished with a mint sprig and lime wheel. Enjoy!

Cucumber Mule

Cucumber in a cocktail is refreshing and perfect for warm weather.

But it also makes me feel like hey there's a vegetable in my drink, this is kinda healthy!

❖ Ingredients

1.5 oz Bombay Sapphire

2 tablespoons Honeydew melon optional

2 slices cucumber sliced lengthwise.

6-8 leaves agave

.5 oz mint can substitute simple syrup.

.75 oz fresh lime juice

1.5 oz Ginger beer

❖ Directions

Step 1: Muddle the cucumber first and then muddle again with the honeydew (optional).

Step 2: Clap the mint and add it to the tin along with the Bombay Sapphire, agave and lime juice.

Step 3: Strain over ice into a Collins glass and top w ginger beer.

Step 4: Garnish with a cucumber ribbon and fresh mint.

Christmas Moscow Mule Cocktail

❖ Ingredients

- 3-4 rosemary needles

- Small pinch of fresh thyme

- **1** teaspoon sugar

- **2** oz vodka

- **2** oz cranberry juice

- **4** oz ginger beer

- Sugar-coated cranberries, for garnish

- Fresh herbs, for garnish

Steps

- In a cocktail shaker, lightly muddle together herbs and sugar. Top with vodka and cranberry juice and shake with ice.

- Strain into a copper cocktail mug and fill with ice and ginger beer. Garnish with cranberries dusted with sugar and fresh herbs.

Frozen Moscow Mules

❖ **Ingredients**

- 3 11.2 ounces ginger beer (three bottles of ginger beer)

- 2 cups vodka

- 12 fluid ounces frozen limeade concentrate

❖ Instructions

- Mix all of the ingredients together in a large freezable container.

- Freeze overnight.

- Let set out for about 20 minutes or until it is easy to scoop. Serve and enjoy!

Holiday Cranberry Mule Recipe

❖ **Ingredients**

- 1.5 oz. Vodka

- 2 oz. Cranberry juice

- Juice of 1 Lime wedge

- Ginger beer (to top)

- Ice cubes

- Fresh or frozen cranberries (for garnish)

- A sprig of Rosemary (for garnish)

❖ How to Make

1. Measure the vodka and cranberry juice with a jigger and pour them into a copper mug.

2. Fill the copper mug with ice cubes and squeeze the lime into it.

3. Top it off with ginger beer. Stir the drink with a bar spoon.

4. Garnish with a handful of cranberries and rosemary.

Spiced Pear Moscow Mule

❖ Ingredients

Spiced Pear Moscow Mule

- 2 ounces vodka

- 1 1/2 ounces spiced pear simple syrup

- 1 ounce fresh lime juice

- 4 ounces ginger beer

Spiced Pear Simple Sugar

- 1 cup pear juice

- 1 cup sugar

- 2 cinnamon sticks

- 3 whole cloves

❖ Instructions

To Make The Cocktail

1. Fill a mug or tall glass with ice. Add the vodka, spiced pear simple syrup, and lime juice. Top with ginger beer. Stir, and garnish with a pear slice and cinnamon stick.

To Make The Simple Syrup

1. Add 1 cup of pear juice, 1 cup of sugar, 2 cinnamon sticks, and 3 whole cloves to a small saucepan. Over medium-high heat, bring the mixture up to a simmer, stirring until the sugar is melted. Turn down the heat and let the syrup simmer for 15 minutes. Remove from heat.

2. Once the mixture is cooled, strain the simple sugar and store it in a jar with a lid. Chill it in the fridge until you're ready to make your Spiced Pear Moscow Mule.

Pomegranate Mule

If the floral note of the hibiscus-berry mule isn't your style, try this pomegranate Moscow mule recipe variation instead. It's just as bold and red but uses the tartness of pomegranate instead of floral hibiscus.

❖ Ingredients

4-5 oz. Ginger beer

1.5 oz. Vodka

½ oz. Pomegranate juice

½ oz. Lime juice

Fresh pomegranate seeds for garnish

Lime wedge for garnish

❖ Directions

Step 1: Combine pomegranate juice, vodka, and lime juice into a copper mug filled with ice.

Step 2: Pour ginger beer over the vodka mixture until the cup is full.

Step 3: Garnish with pomegranate seeds and a lime wedge.

STK Mule

How could we celebrate the Mule by not starting with the original? This version features Smirnoff Vodka with the irresistible kick of ginger.

❖ **Ingredients**

1.5 ounces Belvedere Unfiltered Vodka

1 ounce Chartreuse

1/2-ounce lime juice

Ginger beer

Lime wheel float

Mint sprig

❖ **Directions**

Step 1: Combine vodka, Chartreuse and lime juice in an ice-filled mule mug. Top with ginger beer. Garnish with the lime wheel and a sprig of fresh mint.

Smirnoff Moscow Mule

❖ Ingredients

1 1/2 oz Smirnoff No. 21 Vodka

3 oz Ginger Beer

Squeeze of Fresh Lime Juice

❖ Directions

Step 1: Mix Smirnoff and ginger beer in a copper mug over ice

Step 2: Add a squeeze of lime

Step 3: Garnish with a lime wedge

Non-Alcoholic Moscow Mule

It has lime juice, ginger beer, club soda, and simple syrup (1 part water, 1 part sugar). It's such a crisp and refreshing drink, with the tangy lime juice, and the spicy ginger beer. I liked mine with some mint leaves mixed in too.

❖ Ingredients

1 lime (1-2 tablespoons juice, fresh is best)

1 TBS simple syrup

1/4 cup club soda

3-4 mint leaves (torn, optional)

3/4 cup Ginger Beer (make sure it's nonalcoholic)

Crushed ice

❖ Directions

Step 1: In the bottom of cup, pour juice from lime, simple syrup, and club soda.

Step 2: Add mint leaves if desired.

Step 3: Fill the cup about halfway with ice.

Step 4: The pour about 3/4 a cup of ginger beer over the ice.

Step 5: Garnish with mint leaves and a lime wedge if desired and serve.

Made in United States
Troutdale, OR
04/26/2024

19473731R00046